Incredibly Disgusting Drugs™

Ecstasy

Tamra B. Orr

rosen publishing's
rosen central®

New York

o my children—may they never need to worry about these things

Published in 2008 by The Rosen Publishing Group, Inc.
29 East 21st Street, New York, NY 10010

First Edition

Library of Congress Cataloging-in-Publication Data

Orr, Tamra.
Ecstasy/Tamra Orr.—1st ed.
    p.cm.—(Incredibly disgusting drugs)
Includes bibliographical references and index.
ISBN-13: 978-1-4042-1375-3 (library binding)
1. Ecstasy (Drug) 2. Methamphetamine abuse. 3. Designer drugs. I. Title.
HV5822.M38O77 2008
613.8–dc22

                                                              2007035792

Manufactured in the United States of America

Contents

Introduction

Everybody likes feeling happy. It is great to be filled with the overwhelming belief that all is right with the world. Nothing can stop you. Nothing can get in your way. Destiny, chance, God, karma—they are all with you now. Euphoria is a wonderful place to live.

The drug popularly known as ecstasy can do that for you. It can make you feel loved, content, affectionate, and giddy with the beauty of the moment. But there is a dark and potentially deadly underside to the ecstasy experience. Just look at what happened to Irma, a fourteen-year-old from California. She took her first dose of ecstasy and, in just a few moments, was no longer euphoric. In fact, she was gravely ill. Less than a week later, Irma was taken off life support and her family said good-bye to her forever.

Cathy met a similar fate. She was a senior in high school and was in the middle of planning her wedding.

She had given up drugs a while ago because she was intimidated by the sight of ambulances routinely parked outside her favorite rave club. They were waiting for the drug overdoses that the emergency medical technicians knew would occur throughout the night. Then, prom came around. "Why not make it a little more special with a last ecstasy pill?" Cathy thought. She and thirty-seven fellow classmates did just that. Thirty-seven of them lived. One didn't. Four hours after Cathy took the pill, she went into a coma. Just forty-eight hours later, she was dead. She was buried in her prom dress.

Despite the fact that even the casual use of ecstasy can lead to death, people keep taking it. The good news is that recent reports say ecstasy use is down from its height in the late 1990s and early 2000s. The bad news is that the numbers are still too high. Steven Pasierb, the president and CEO of the Partnership for a Drug-Free America, told CNN.com, "Even though we have the good news that overall ecstasy use has leveled off after a big surge, we've still got 55 percent of teenagers—13 million American teenagers—who say they see no great risk in trying it. And that's what we have to reverse." In 2005, more than 502,000 people aged twelve and over reported having used ecstasy in the past month. In 2006, 1.4 percent of the nation's eighth graders, 2.8 percent of all tenth graders, and 4.1 percent of all twelfth graders had tried it.

Where did ecstasy come from in the first place? No one set out to create it. Its discovery was actually a mistake. In 1913, Merck, a German

The worry over ecstasy made national headlines when *Time* magazine's June 5, 2000, edition examined what it is doing to our nation and its youth.

pharmaceutical company, was trying to synthesize a new medicine. The drug that has come to be known as ecstasy was an unexpected by-product. It was called 3, 4 methylene-dioxymethamphetamine, or MDMA for short. Now that the research chemists had it, what were they supposed to do with it? Some studies have shown the drug was initially used as an appetite suppressant, but others disagree. They claim it was used briefly in the 1950s by the military as a type of truth serum.

It was not until the 1970s, however, that someone tried to use it for recreation, or "just for fun." Ten years later, it became a tool for psychiatrists and therapists to help their patients get in touch with emotions that they had repressed and were struggling to express. Soon after, it became the drug of choice among college students.

In 1985, the U.S. Drug Enforcement Administration (DEA) decided that ecstasy was a danger to the public. Under a new law, it was able to place an emergency ban on it. Despite objections from those who used the pill in conjunction with their mental health therapy, ecstasy was declared a Schedule 1 drug, which meant it was deemed to have no medical value and it carried serious risks, including brain damage. It was now illegal to make, use, or sell ecstasy. Two years later, ecstasy began to spread throughout England, then Australia, and ultimately the United States, despite the ban. It became a favorite at raves, or all-night dance parties.

Today, ecstasy is a drug that is sure to worry parents, frustrate physicians, and tempt young people. The bottom line is, while ecstasy can make you feel that all is right with the world, it can also make your world come crashing down around you.

The 1
Dangerous and
Dirty Business
of Making Ecstasy

When you look at a hit, or dose, of ecstasy, it is hard to imagine that it could be dangerous. After all, it often comes in pill form, and the pills are stamped with a smiley face or some other harmless-looking character. It may even have a butterfly, heart, clover, or Zodiac sign on it. Surely, this is just a young adult version of a children's vitamin?

Not by a long shot. Ecstasy is really 3, 4 methylene-dioxymethamphetamine (MDMA). Unlike some other drugs, it is entirely synthetic, or human-made. Although it mainly comes in the form of a white, yellow, or brown pill, it is occasionally produced in powder form for snorting up your nose as well. It can be turned into a liquid to be injected in an arm or leg. As if this were not glamorous enough, ecstasy can also be made into a suppository and inserted into the anus in a drug delivery method known as "shafting."

How can pills that remind you of the vitamins you took as a kid be so toxic? Don't let their cute, whimsical looks fool you. These pills can kill you.

The size, dosage, color, and appearance of ecstasy pills vary, depending on where they were made. A typical tablet contains 80 to 150 milligrams of MDMA and costs the user $10 to $25 each. If someone offers a lower price, it is likely that the pills are impure and contain additives ranging from cough syrup to rat poison.

Mixing a Lethal Brew

Because MDMA is illegal to use, buy, sell, or manufacture in the United States, it cannot be made in legitimate labs. The majority of it is produced in the Netherlands and Belgium, where it is also illegal. It is then smuggled into the United States through either the postal system or on airline flights.

Not all ecstasy arrives from foreign countries, though. Some of it is made secretly in this country in trailers, barns, motel rooms, houseboats, mini-storage units, basements, kitchens, and home labs. The ingredients are few, so they are easy to pile into a large suitcase or other container in case the manufacturers have to move quickly to avoid getting caught.

A **Drug** by Any **Other Name**

MDMA, or ecstasy, has many different names. Here are the most common ones:

Club drug	X
Hug	Beans
Clarity	Love drug
Lover's speed	Roll
Ecstasy	Disco biscuits
Adam	The Experience
XTC	New Yorker

Although the manufacturing of ecstasy seems relatively easy, it actually requires a good understanding of chemistry to be able to pull it off. The necessary chemicals are not always easy to find. It is not a simple procedure, nor is it a very safe one. A single mistake can result in dangerous situations, like toxic fume leaks or even lethal explosions. Since many of the drug's makers are not trained chemists but simply drug traffickers and users who are using ecstasy "recipes" found on the Internet, mistakes and accidents are quite common. A police officer in North Carolina recalls an arrest of some of these "self-taught cooks." He told InTheKnowZone.com, "They got the directions out of books and stuff, but if they'd turned to the

Sharing drug supplies at raves and other clubs may seem generous, but what happens when the person you share with goes to the hospital? Will you be sharing the medical expenses as well? Or the jail time?

wrong page of something, they could have mixed the wrong things and killed people."

Sadly, sometimes these self-made cooks are not even adults. In November 2001, four curious young boys in Scotland went surfing on the Internet and found a recipe for homemade ecstasy. "Teenage boys will be tempted to experiment, and it is a cause of great concern that

Police officers search through 463 pounds of materials used to make ecstasy in a warehouse in the Netherlands. It was one of the largest synthetic drug busts in the country's history. Police seized 2.5 million tablets and enough raw materials to make 8 million more.

such information should be on the 'Net," school spokesman Jeremy Poulter told the BBC. When the boys took their own homemade treats, they all became so ill that they were rushed to the hospital and later expelled from school.

Your
Body on
Ecstasy

Just what happens when ecstasy enters the body? A lot! The more often the drug is used and the higher the doses, the more powerful the effects. Keep doing it, and the risk to your body just grows and grows.

Imagine for a moment that you have decided to try some ecstasy. You go ahead and swallow the pill. What happens next? For the first twenty to thirty minutes or so, nothing seems to happen. After an hour, however, you become very aware that something is changing inside of you. For the next twenty minutes, your emotions will continue to climb upward like a roller coaster cresting the highest peak. Then, for the next two to three hours, you will stay there at the top. It is a plateau that you think you would like to remain on forever and ever. What could possibly be wrong with something that feels this good?

Although you may feel completely relaxed and at one with the world, your muscles know otherwise.

They become tense from your head to your toes. You feel very alert, aware of absolutely everything. Your teeth are grinding, and your jaws are clenching. You chew on your cheeks or tongue. Of course, you do not notice any of this because you are too busy feeling great about the world and everything and everyone in it.

Dehydration and Organ Stress

You feel energized. You feel as if you can do anything and that everything will work out great. But no one told your internal thermostat that. Ecstasy wreaks havoc on the system that controls your body temperature. You cannot cool off. You may be dancing or bouncing around—after all, you can do anything right now! However, as you enjoy your newfound energy, your body is heating up inside.

Your temperature can easily spike to more than 100 degrees Fahrenheit (37.8 degrees Celsius) or higher. Some ecstasy users have run temperatures of 108 (42.2 degrees Celsius) degrees before they began to literally melt from the inside out. This is called "bleeding out." All of the water in your body gets used up within minutes. High temperatures damage the liver and the kidney, perhaps permanently or even fatally. Your cardiovascular system begins to fail. Your heart rate and blood pressure are already soaring way above normal.

The pressure being exerted on your body by this high temperature, dehydration, and organ stress is immense. Your pulse rate may double or triple. If you happen to already have high blood pressure, heart disease, diabetes, epilepsy, or panic attacks, the stress placed on your body

Sprawling on the floor to feel ecstasy's kick is common in raves. The drug's users celebrate their growing maturity by lying down on the floor, zoning out, and sucking on candy pacifiers, all the while risking serious and permanent brain damage.

will be even greater, and the effects more severe and dangerous. You may have chills or excessive sweating, but heck, you still feel terrific, right? In actuality, you are on the verge of heatstroke—the primary cause of death from ecstasy use. "When the body overheats enough," says Ted Mills, researcher at the National Heart, Lung, and Blood Institute, "skeletal muscle breaks down and organs fail, leading to an agonizing death."

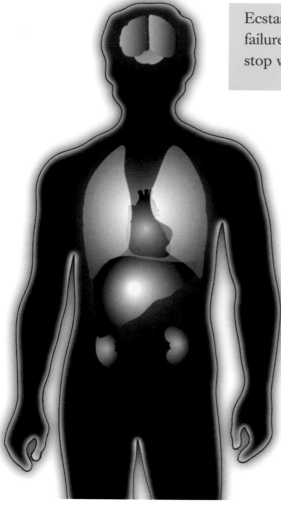

Ecstasy users risk heart failure. During heart failure, the lungs fill up with fluid, the kidneys stop working, and the brain hemorrhages.

Mixing Alcohol and Ecstasy

Perhaps you decide to drink something while you are dancing. After all, you are hot and thirsty. Since ecstasy can make your body dehydrate quickly, that seems like a wise idea. Plus, won't drinking something help to keep your body temperature down? No. What are you drinking? If you are like most young people, it is not water. Often it is soda, but too many times it is alcohol. Alcohol and ecstasy are the perfect combination if you are bent on self-destruction.

Alcohol dehydrates the body, right along with the ecstasy. Mary Jo Desprez, associate director of Eastern Michigan University's health program, personally witnessed this when one of the school's students combined alcohol and ecstasy and died. "It's never possible to know the effect of alcohol and drug combinations," she explained to Echo Online. "There can be extreme consequences. One of the primary dangers in taking either of these drugs by themselves is the chance of dehydration. [Taken] together, the dehydration effect is compounded, and the risk is higher. Further, MDMA decreases the body's ability to regulate body temperature and alcohol can raise body temperature, increasing chances of death by hypertension."

Water Intoxication

So, drink water instead, right? Once again, it sounds like a smart idea, but often it is not. A young woman named Leah Betts provides a cautionary example of why water and ecstasy do not mix. She took some ecstasy in 1995, and when she got hot, she began drinking a lot of water. She had heard that was the best thing to counteract the dehydrating effects of the drug. However, ecstasy can cause a condition known as hyponatremia, or water intoxication. The drug, which has deprived your body of the water it so desperately needs, now interferes with the body's ability to metabolize water. It causes the body to release a hormone that slows down the functioning of the kidneys—the organs most involved in handling liquids.

Betts was celebrating her eighteenth birthday and decided to add ecstasy to the fun. After she got hot and started drinking the water, she then lapsed into a coma. Autopsy results say she died because of brain swelling. If a person drinks a lot of water but cannot metabolize it quickly enough, the blood becomes diluted. What does the body do to cope? The water is sucked into brain cells, making them swell up. Pressure builds on

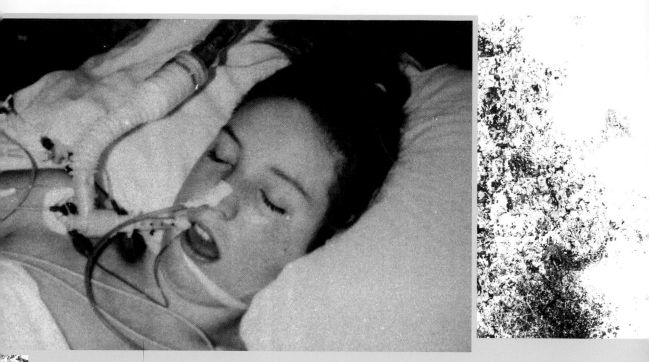

Leah Betts turned eighteen and then never had the chance to celebrate another birthday. Ecstasy was her birthday present, and death was the result.

the brain stem, and the person is soon in a coma and then dead. Dr. John Henry, director of the National Poisons Unit in England, said, "[Leah] drank a lot of water, but with a lack of understanding of why she needed to drink water. Water is not an antidote to ecstasy; it is an antidote to dancing."

Clenching and Chewing

One of the more gruesome physical side effects of ecstasy use is what it does to your teeth. Ecstasy makes users grind their teeth and clench their

Ed Thanhouser sucks on a pacifier at a rave in Oregon. Is this the mature and attractive look you want to present to others?

jaws, resulting in serious damage. Teeth enamel gets cracked, and the teeth are worn down. The jaws get strained and may become misaligned. Many people attempt to protect themselves from these side effects by chewing gum or sucking on lollipops and plastic or candy pacifiers. Yet, the act of sucking and the sugary nature of these candies are also harmful to teeth. "If someone uses pacifiers, it can cause orthodontic problems," dentist Steven Cohen told Metroactive.com. "If you hold it in the front and it pushes on the front teeth, it has the effect of thumb sucking. With all of that sugar, lollipops are even worse."

A study conducted in Britain showed that 60 percent of ecstasy users examined had bruxism and had worn their teeth through the enamel and beyond. Dr. Hal Crossley is one dentist who has seen the harm that ecstasy has done to young people's teeth. He travels all over North America lecturing about the effects of ecstasy on users and their teeth. "I'm not your average dentist," he told Metroactive.com. "I've seen users who have ground their teeth down to nubs. Their molars become flat, polished stumps. The back teeth go, and then the front teeth are just ground right down. The enamel in the front just dissolves away."

While grinding damages teeth, the harmful effects of ecstasy on your mouth and teeth do not stop there. Users frequently have a dry mouth and use soft drinks to wet their throats and cool off. These drinks often are brimming with sugar. Other people react to the drug by vomiting, and the stomach acid that comes up eats at the enamel on teeth. All of these result in dental nightmares. "What we've found is with any type of amphetamine, it brings anxiety, tension, clenching, and grinding," said Cohen. "It can cause broken and cracked teeth and nerve damage in the teeth, which can lead to root canals. And people who use a lot of drugs don't usually put dental hygiene as a top priority."

Other Dangers of Ecstasy Use

The harm that ecstasy use can cause the body does not stop at the teeth. Just one hit of ecstasy can cause:

- Blurred vision
- Nausea and vomiting
- Faintness
- Erectile dysfunction
- Headache
- Vertigo
- Acnelike rash
- Tremors
- Heart attack
- Seizures
- Brain cell destruction

Not only can your body experience serious damage due to ecstasy use but so can your mind, as we will see in the next chapter.

Your
Brain on
Ecstasy

cstasy does some ugly physical damage to a person's body, but what about the less easily observed effects that it has on you? How does this drug affect your mind and personality? Ask Dr. Karl Jansen, an expert at the antidrug Web site Ecstasy.org, and his answer is scary, sobering, and absolutely honest. "Like other potent mind-altering drugs, the use of ecstasy has been associated with impaired mental health and impaired judgment," he told a writer from Narconon of Southern California. "While under the influence of the drug, users may sometimes experience confusion, disorientation, anxiety, panic attacks, depression, insomnia, deperson-alization, derealization, perceptual disorders and hallucinations, paranoia, and psychotic phenomena. Suffice to say, it is extremely dangerous."

Clearly, ecstasy can make a person feel pretty terrific while taking it, at least initially. You feel comfortable and

The National Institute on Drug Abuse recently launched a new national public service campaign on what drugs do to the brain. Director Dr. Alan I. Leshner points to pictures illustrating ecstasy's effects on the brain.

content. You feel powerfully connected to others. Everyone seems like your new best friend and soul mate. Inhibitions are reduced, and the need to touch other people is increased—a combination that can lead to a lot of regrets later. It can result in having sex with someone whom you normally would not choose to be with, possibly without proper protection against AIDS, other sexually transmitted diseases, or pregnancy.

Poor Choices, Mounting Problems

Ecstasy can make you feel emotionally open, ready to spill your guts about every secret you have to anyone who will listen, possibly to someone who is not truly your friend and who may not be trustworthy or have your best interests at stake. Although emotional honesty and accessibility can be a good thing in some situations, it may not be if it is offered to the wrong person at the wrong time.

Sharing personal thoughts and problems should only be done after you have carefully decided to do so. A sudden release of these emotional issues can be hard to handle—for you and for whomever you are confessing to. Later, after the drug has worn off, you may regret every word you said and every action you took. As Mary Jo Desprez of Eastern Michigan University told Echo Online, "The biggest problem with alcohol and other drugs is that the first thing it takes away is our ability to make reasoned judgments. Something that probably wouldn't sound like a good idea doesn't sound so bad under the influence. And if everybody in a group has been drinking and someone starts to take another drug, there's really not anybody in that group who can tell them it's not such a good idea."

Time becomes distorted when under the influence of ecstasy. If you have to be someplace on time—home, work, school, or elsewhere—you may never make it there. Ecstasy commonly makes it hard to concentrate for more than a few minutes. Your mind may wander—a true problem if you happen to be behind the wheel of a car or trying to do some aspect

Couples may start out going to a rave for the dancing but end up dosing instead. Ecstasy often leads to unplanned and unprotected sex with a casual date or a partner you may not even know or remember.

of your job. All of this can lead to problems at school and at work, possibly resulting in you losing friends, flunking out, getting kicked off of teams or out of extracurricular clubs, or getting fired.

Damaged Mood Regulators

Deep inside the brain, ecstasy is scrambling things around, especially when it comes to serotonin. Serotonin is a chemical messenger that plays a very important role in regulating people's moods, as well as their sexual activity, their sleep, and their sensitivity to pain. Ecstasy causes the body to release abnormally high amounts of serotonin, hence the feeling of well-being.

The neurons, or brain cells, that store serotonin, however, are deformed or destroyed when this happens. Research has shown that people who use the drug more than twenty-five times have lowered serotonin levels for as long as a year after quitting. Lowered serotonin levels are associated with depression and poor sleep. Therefore, ecstasy can ultimately make you feel the opposite of ecstatic, as that illusory euphoria and sense of well-being evaporates after a few hours or less.

Can these damaged or destroyed neurons ever grow back? Sometimes, but if they do, they often develop abnormally or in the wrong places. This further interferes with your body's ability to produce serotonin and another mood-regulating chemical called dopamine, which is in charge of the pleasure and addiction centers of the brain. The pill wears off, the dopamine and serotonin are depleted, and you are left feeling depressed.

The Day After: Short-Term Effects

As great as you may feel after taking ecstasy, the payback can be brutal. It may not hit for a few hours or even the next day, but rest assured, it will hit. Prepare for the coming crash. It won't be pretty.

Remember those depleted amounts of serotonin and dopamine discussed previously? Without any of those in your brain, you are

From the Front Lines

What do some ecstasy users say about the drug? "I know people who have taken it every day for long periods of time, and they're not the same person anymore. It makes you a zombie after you do it too much," one eighteen-year-old user told ConnectWithKids.com. Daniel, a former user, said, "I'd tell them, 'Get out while you can. It starts out all fun, games, and parties, but it leads to real nasty things. You become your own worst enemy.'"

almost guaranteed a serious dose of can't-get-out-of-bed, life-has-no-meaning-anymore depression. You will be tired—sometimes so tired that you will not be able to go to work or school. For some, this fatigue lasts a few hours. Others take a full day to recover. For still others, it can last for more than a week. You lose an entire week for a couple of hours' high. What kind of trade-off is that?

It doesn't stop there. One recent study cited by Narconon of Southern California shows that the negative side effects of ecstasy carried over into one's personal life in astounding ways. "Users reported financial problems (39 percent), relationship or social problems (39 percent), and occupational and study problems (38 percent)," the study states. Taking ecstasy, like taking so many other drugs, is like tossing a stone into water. You just cannot imagine how far the ripples will extend, or for how long.

Following a dose of ecstasy, your appetite may disappear. You may have trouble concentrating. It is common to be confused, anxious, and paranoid. Sleeping may be difficult, and you may start craving additional drugs. Just think of what this will do to your life at home, work, and school. How will it change your friendships? What fun will you be to hang around with?

Use ecstasy too often and you may experience dizziness, blackouts, and even death. Many frequent users report that after the first ten times or so, the pills lose their "magic." The sad result is that many users take even more ecstasy to recapture the lost euphoria, further damaging their minds and bodies in the process.

Coming down from ecstasy may send you into depths of depression you did not even know existed before.

Long-Term Damage

Whether or not ecstasy causes any lasting brain damage has been the subject of endless debate. A study entitled "Severe Dopaminergic Neurotoxicity in Primates After a Common Recreational Dose Regimen of MDMA (Ecstasy)" was published in *Science Magazine* in 2002 and claimed that it did. The researcher and author, Dr. George A. Ricaurte, said that he had proved it, but problems with the research were discovered later and the study's results were invalidated. Soon after, article after article appeared in magazines and newspapers stating that claims of ecstasy-related brain damage were all false, that ecstasy was not nearly as dangerous as some had thought after all. Too many people used this as a convenient excuse to become users again.

Today, research on this issue continues. So far, the news is not good. It looks like ecstasy can cause brain damage, even for first-time users. "Most people will think, 'When I use it heavily and when I use it frequently, it's not good for my brain. But when I take it a few times, it doesn't really harm me,'" Dr. Maartje De Win, researcher at the University of Amsterdam, told Chicago's CBS affiliate. New evidence reveals that this may not be the case, however. A recent study shows that people who took no more than six tablets over an eighteen-month period experienced changes in their brains, including obvious brain cell damage and memory problems. "We found a decrease in blood circulation in some areas of the brain in young adults who just started to use ecstasy," Dr. De Win said in a separate interview with the Canadian Broadcasting Corporation (CBC). "In addition, we found a relative

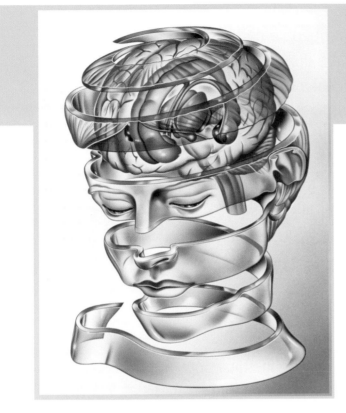

The hippocampus is the large purple oval on the right, and its main function is memory. Ecstasy use can make it hard to learn and remember anything.

decrease in verbal memory performance in ecstasy users compared to nonusers."

Another study published by the American Academy of Neurology states that long-term ecstasy use definitely interferes with memory. Apparently, the hippocampus—the part of the brain associated with learning and new memory—is impaired. Dr. Konstantine Zakzanis, professor at the University of Toronto's Division of Life Sciences, said, "For those who use ecstasy repeatedly, there is preliminary evidence to suggest memory processes can be impaired with continued use of the drug." What about those who use it only once or twice? "To date, there is no evidence to suggest impairment of memory function that is progressive or permanent in nature, although the jury of ecstasy researchers are still deliberating the matter," he stated.

Your brain cannot be replaced. It cannot be put in a cast until it is healed. It is not a spare part that people can live without. Instead, it is the master of the entire body. "You do not want to do anything that is going to damage your brain because that is one area of your body that does not regenerate. It does not fix itself," said addiction counselor Dr. Robert Margolis.

Is the brain damage associated with ecstasy use permanent? No one is sure yet. Research and studies continue to try and find out, but in the meantime, why would anyone want to take the risk? "We do not know if these effects are transient or permanent," added Dr. De Win in the CBC interview. "Therefore, we cannot conclude that ecstasy, even in small doses, is safe for the brain, and people should be informed of this risk."

Is Ecstasy Addictive?

So, is ecstasy actually addictive? It depends on whom you ask. It has not yet been proven to be physically addictive. Some scientists are convinced that it is, while others think it is highly unlikely. Psychological addiction, however, is something else altogether. You are considered to be psychologically addicted to a drug if you continue to use it despite your knowledge of its harmful side effects.

It is easy to understand why someone might become emotionally addicted to ecstasy. If the person has a rough life, the pill gives him or her a happier outlook, at least temporarily. If the person is depressed, he or she experiences a brief moment of joy and peace. The tablet brings a much-needed release or escape from a harsh reality.

However, the price for these isolated moments of false well-being is simply too high. The toll it takes on your body is powerful. The cost to your brain may be irreparable. As the U.S. Drug Enforcement Administration (DEA) says on its Web site, "This isn't a game you can win: You can cheat on your boyfriend, cheat on your taxes, even cheat death . . . but you just can't beat your own biology (at least in this case). The user that seeks frequent escape in MDMA will be ground down; the problems they sought to escape will only be made worse by frequent use."

In other words, the high that comes with ecstasy will only make the lows lower, the depression deeper, and the frustration with reality more intense and intolerable. Ecstasy is not an answer. It will instead become just another source of stress to add to your ever-growing list of problems.

4

A World of Trouble in One Small Pill

Taking a drug that can make the world go away and leave you floating in a kind of euphoria may sound tempting, but take a minute to think a little more critically about this. Scientists have confirmed the very real short-term damage that ecstasy causes, but they are still learning about the potential long-term damage the drug can do to your mind and body. Are you willing to take the risk just so you can feel better for a couple of hours? The potential price is simply too steep.

To complicate matters, an ecstasy pill may contain more than MDMA. Why? Keep in mind who is making this stuff. It is not the professional pharmaceutical labs that have strict safety guidelines, detailed directions to follow, quality control, licensed and certified technicians, and sanitary lab conditions. These are amateurs working in secret, often filthy labs making illegal substances in a big hurry. Many of the people making ecstasy are not nearly educated or experienced enough to know

A drug raid in Brazil turns up enough chemistry supplies to make more than 10,000 tablets. The owner of the lab escaped arrest.

what they are doing. They found a recipe on the Internet or through a friend who was told by a neighbor how to make it. They then try to do so from memory. These amateur drug manufacturers want to make ecstasy quickly and cheaply, and sell it for as much as they can get. With these motivations in mind, your health and safety are completely irrelevant to them. So, they skimp on the MDMA and add potentially dangerous or toxic filler to increase their profit. It's all in the name of good business, right?

What do they add, you ask? These ecstasy pills often contain other dangerous and illegal drugs, such as speed, PCP (angel dust), and LSD (acid). They also contain ephedrine or caffeine, ingredients guaranteed to speed your heart rate up and dehydrate you even more. Aspirin might be in there or atropine, a drug that relaxes the muscles lining the intestines. Prepare to be close to a bathroom or have an embarrassing accident! An anesthetic called ketamine can be in there, as well as a potent hallucinogen known as paramethoxyamphetamine. Typically, tablets will have thirteen to fourteen times more dextromethorphan than is used in cough suppressant. Some manufacturers of ecstasy even throw in rat poison, adding to an already toxic mixture.

Is there any way to make sure an ecstasy pill you have bought and are about to swallow is safe? Not really. There are home kits you can buy to test the pills, as well as Web sites devoted to telling you how to test them for purity. The problem is that all these kits do is tell you if there is MDMA in the pill and how much. They will not tell you what else is in there. So, you will find out if you've been ripped off, but not if you might die if you go ahead and take the pill. What kind of rush are you going to get from a pill that contains some of these additives? It just might be a rush to the hospital—or the morgue.

Herbal Ecstasy

You eat only organic vegetables. You take vitamins. You shop at natural food stores and buy organic dietary supplements. Therefore, maybe you think the Cloud 9, Herbal Bliss, Ritual Spirit, or Herbal XTC is a better choice than chemical ecstasy. Watch out! These "all-natural," "herbal" "health supplements" contain caffeine and ephedrine, in addition to other substances that can cause serious side effects, including brain damage.

Getting Caught

You can damage your body with ecstasy. You can mess up your mind. You can even die. But what happens if you get caught with an illegal substance like ecstasy?

Since ecstasy is in the same drug classification as heroin and cocaine, you will be arrested. If you are older than sixteen, your name will be published in the newspaper. You will also get a criminal record that will follow you throughout life, for instance when you fill out college applications, apply for jobs, try to buy a house, and seek loans or health and life insurance. Your mug shot is taken to add to your criminal history sheet, and it may become available to the public, possibly even ending up on the Internet.

If you were driving at the time of your arrest, your car will be impounded, as well as anything that is in it, including illegal drugs. Even if some of the substances are not yours, you will still be charged with possession of them. If you are charged with the possession of one ecstasy tablet, you face up to a year in prison, or a $1,000 fine and three years probation. You may also have to attend a drug rehab program.

Is It an Overdose?

Recognizing the signs of an ecstasy overdose is very important. Too many kids have become seriously ill or have died because their friends were not paying close enough attention to their symptoms. Here are the most common ones:

- Feeling hot
- Headache
- Not able to sweat
- Can't control
   body movements
- Confusion
- Vomiting
- Racing heart
- Tremors

- Can't talk properly
- Fainting
- Trouble urinating
- Feeling unwell
- High blood pressure
- Muscle cramping
- Seizures
- Panic attacks

A single dose of ecstasy can cause an overdose. Ask Sridhar Natarajan, chief medical examiner for Lubbock, Texas. He once had to perform an autopsy on a sixteen-year-old boy named Thomas Mallory. Natarajan told the local television channel KCBD, "These drugs are so dangerous, they can cause death just by taking them. They don't have to reach a certain level. What may be lethal to one person might not be to another."

Could Mallory have been saved if his friends had been paying closer attention to his symptoms of ecstasy-related illness? It is quite possible. Attorney Jonathan Stark told KCBD that the blame lies with multiple people, including the person who gave the boy the drug and the friends who were with him and did not immediately get him medical care. "[They] thought it more important to protect their status, privileges, and allowances than [to] get their friend help. [They] left him to die in the seventeenth fairway of the golf course."

Friends of Nicole Crowder, who died after taking ecstasy, put up a sign to show their feelings. They had to take it down until the school found a healthy outlet for their grief.

Don't let this happen to you or to one of your friends. Here is what to do if you or someone you are with begins showing signs of a drug overdose:

• Call 911. State your name and location and be very honest and specific about any drugs or alcohol that your friend has used, including when and how much.
• Stay with your friend until help arrives.
• If your friend is still conscious, have him/her sit up so that when he/she vomits, he/she will not choke.
• If unconscious, roll your friend on his or her side to help prevent choking on vomit or the tongue, and stay there until the ambulance arrives.

Are you worried that your friend will be upset about you reporting his or her drug use? Think again. You are saving your friend's life. In the worst-case scenario, it is better to lose a friend than for that friend to lose his or her life.

Former ecstasy users Dayna Moore and Philip McCarthy testify before the Senate Governmental Affairs Committee in Washington in 2001. On this national public stage, they shared their ecstasy horror stories.

Ecstasy is often defined as a state of bliss or extreme happiness. A tablet may bring you that feeling, but it is like the awe-inspiring stillness and hush before a damaging tornado hits. It may feel nice right now, but soon you could be overwhelmed by long-term depression, illness, mental deterioration, and hospitalization. You may even face death. Once spent, you may never be able to get your physical, mental, and emotional health back. As a consequence, a genuine feeling of real and natural ecstasy will forever be beyond your grasp.

Glossary

atropine A poisonous alkaloid made from the belladonna plant (deadly nightshade) that is used to relieve spasms. It can cause hallucinations, nausea, dizziness, blurred vision, heart-racing, and extreme confusion.

bruxism Grinding of the teeth.

by-product A secondary result, often unexpected or unintended.

caffeine An alkaloid found in such things as coffee, tea, and cola that acts as a stimulant.

dehydrate To remove water from the body; to lose water.

dextromethorphan A nonaddictive cough suppressant or syrup. It is often found in fake ecstasy pills and, in high doses, can cause hallucinations, nausea, sweating, fever, hypertension, dizziness, vomiting, diarrhea, difficulty urinating, high blood pressure, and elevated heart rate.

dopamine A neurotransmitter in the central nervous system that regulates movement and emotion and is implicated in the onset of Parkinson's disease, a neurological disorder.

ephedrine An alkaloid used for the treatment of asthma and hay fever. It also acts as a stimulant and appetite suppressant and can cause hypertension, flushing, sweating, nausea, increased or difficult urination, restlessness, anxiety, panic, dizziness, tremors, and fainting.

hallucinogen A substance that produces hallucinations or intense imaginary visions.

hippocampus A part of the brain that deals with memory retention.

hyponatremia A lack of sodium in the blood (often due to the intake of large amounts of water).

ketamine A general anesthetic used in surgery. It is often used illegally for its sedative and hallucinogenic properties but can cause brain damage and other health problems.

LSD (lysergic acid diethylamide) A powerful psychedelic drug that produces hallucinations.

neuron An impulse-conducting cell that functions in the nervous system.

paramethoxyamphetamine (PMA) A hallucinogen.

PCP Often referred to as "angel dust;" a hallucinogen.

rave Originally a British term for a place to dance all night long; an all-night dance party.

serotonin A neurotransmitter that is involved in sleep, depression, and memory.

speed Any stimulating drug, usually an amphetamine.

suppository A capsule of medicine inserted in either the anus or vagina.

suppressant Something that stops an undesirable action or condition.

synthesize To form by combining separate parts or elements into a whole.

synthetic Artificial; human-made.

American Council for Drug Education
164 West 74th Street
New York, NY 10023
(800) 488-DRUG
Web site: http://www.acde.org
The American Council for Drug Education is a substance abuse prevention and education agency that develops programs and materials based on the most current scientific research on drug use and its impact on society.

Canadian Centre on Substance Abuse (CCSA)
75 Albert Street, Suite 300
Ottawa, ON K1P SE7
Canada
(613) 235-4048
Web site: http://www.ccsa.ca/ccsa
CCSA has a legislated mandate to provide national leadership and evidence-informed analysis and advice to mobilize collaborative efforts to reduce alcohol and other drug-related harms.

National Council on Alcoholism and Drug Dependence (NCADD)
244 East 58th Street, 4th Floor
New York, NY 10022

(212) 269-7797

Web site: http://www.ncadd.org

NCADD provides education, information, help, and hope to the public. It advocates addiction prevention, intervention, and treatment through a nationwide network of affiliates. In addition, NCADD operates a toll-free Hope Line (800-NCA-CALL) for information and referral, and a National Intervention Network (800-654-HOPE) to educate and assist the families and friends of addicted persons.

National Institute on Drug Abuse (NIDA)

6001 Executive Boulevard, Room 5213

Bethesda, MD 20892-9561

Web site: http://www.nida.nih.gov

NIDA's mission is to bring the power of science to bear on drug abuse and addiction by supporting and conducting research across a broad range of disciplines and ensuring the rapid and effective dissemination and use of the results of that research to significantly improve prevention, treatment, and policy as it relates to drug abuse and addiction.

Web Sites

Due to the changing nature of Internet links, Rosen Publishing has developed an online list of Web sites related to the subject of this book. This site is updated regularly. Please use this link to access the list:

http://www.rosenlinks.com/idd/ecst

For Further Reading

Bankston, John. *Ecstasy=Busted!* Berkeley Heights, NJ: Enslow Publishers, 2005.

Connolly, Sean. *Ecstasy: Straight Talking*. Mankato, MN: Smart Apple Media, 2006.

Elliot-Wright, Susan. *Amphetamines and Ecstasy*. Chicago, IL: Raintree, 2005.

Fitzhugh, Karla. *Ecstasy: What's the Deal?* Chicago, IL: Heinemann, 2005.

Lane, Stephanie. *Drug Education Library: Ecstasy*. San Diego, CA: Lucent Books, 2005.

Levert, Suzanne. *The Facts About Ecstasy*. Salt Lake City, UT: Benchmark Books, 2004.

Schroeder, Brock, and David J. Triggle. *Ecstasy*. New York, NY: Chelsea House Publications, 2003.

Smith, Lynn Marie. *Rolling Away: My Agony with Ecstasy*. New York, NY: Washington Square Press, 2006.

Weatherly, Myra. *Ecstasy and Other Designer Drug Dangers*. Berkeley Heights, NJ: Enslow Publishers, 2001.

Werther, Scott P. *Ecstasy and Your Heart: The Incredibly Disgusting Story*. New York, NY: Rosen Publishing, 2001.

Wurtzel, Elizabeth. *More, Now, Again: A Memoir of Addiction*. New York, NY: Simon & Schuster, 2001.

Bibliography

"Addiction." DEA.org. Retrieved August 2007 (http://thedea.org/technicalFAQ.html).

"Autopsy Report Shows Teen Died of Ecstasy Overdose." KCBD News Channel 11. July 26, 2005. Retrieved August 2007 (http://www.kcbd.com/Global/story.asp?S=3644668).

"Cathy's Prom." Voice of the Victims. August 31, 2005. Retrieved August 2007 (http://www.cathysprom.com/cathy's_story7.htm).

Childers, Mary Ann. "Ecstasy Can Cause Brain Damage in First-Time Users." CBS Chicago. November 27, 2006. Retrieved August 2007 (http://cbs2chicago.com/health/local_story_331213026.html).

D'Angelo, Laura. "'E' Is for Empty: Daniel's Story." NIDA for Teens. May 21, 2006. Retrieved August 2007 (http://teens.drugabuse.gov/stories/story_xtc1.asp).

"Ecstasy Myths." Drugscope.org. Retrieved August 2007 (http://www.drugscope.org.uk/resources/mediaguide/ecstasymyths.htm).

"Ecstasy 'Relieves Parkinson's Disease.'" BBC News. February 14, 2001. Retrieved August 2007 (http://news.bbc.co.uk/1/hi/health/1169980.stm).

"Ecstasy Study Shock." Narconon of Southern California. Retrieved August 2007 (http://www.ecstasy.ws/user-news.htm?id=118).

"Final Autopsy Shows Drugs Killed Lubbock Teen." KCBD News Channel 11. July 26, 2005. Retrieved August 2007 (http://www.kcbd.com/Global/story.asp?S=3644019&nav=CcXHcbMf).

Gahlinger, Paul. *Illegal Drugs: A Complete Guide to Their History, Chemistry, Use, and Abuse.* New York, NY: Plume, 2003.

Halevy, Emily. "Ecstasy Linked to Brain Damage." ConnectWithKids.com. June 13, 2007. Retrieved August 2007 (http://www.connectwithkids.com/tipsheet/2007/337_jun13/thisweek/070613_ecstasy.shtml).

"It Can't Happen to Me." DEA Street Smart Prevention. 2006. Retrieved August 2007 (http://www.justthinktwice.com/itcant/irma.cfm).

Julien, Robert M. *A Primer of Drug Action: A Concise, Non-Technical Guide to the Actions, Uses, and Side Effects of Psychoactive Drugs.* New York, NY: Owl Books, 2001.

Kuhn, Cynthia, Scott Swartzwelder, and Wilkie Wilson. *Buzzed: The Straight Facts About the Most Used and Abused Drugs from Alcohol to Ecstasy.* New York, NY: W. W. Norton & Co., 2003.

Laurance, Jeremy. "Leah Betts Died of Drinking Water to Counter Drug's Effects." *Times of London.* November 22, 1995. Retrieved August 2007 (http://www.urban75.com/Drugs/drugxtc1.html).

"New Information on Ecstasy Deaths." Narconon of Southern California. Retrieved August 2007 (http://www.ecstasy.ws/user-news.htm?id=86).

Oehmke, Ted. "The Poisoning of Suburbia." Salon.com. July 6, 2000. Retrieved August 2007 (http://archive.salon.com/health/feature/2000/07/06/pma).

Philipkoski, Kristen. "Does Ecstasy Cause Parkinson's?" *Wired*. September 27, 2002. Retrieved August 2007 (http://www. wired.com/medtech/health/news/2002/09/55427).

"Pupils Expelled Over Internet Ecstasy." BBC.com. November 7, 2001. Retrieved August 2007 (http://news.bbc.co.uk/2/hi/uk_news/ scotland/1642646.stm).

Schrader, Jessica. "Alcohol, Ecstasy Can Be Lethal Combination." Echo Online. January 5, 2005. Retrieved August 2007 (http://www. easternecho.com).

"Small Doses of Ecstasy Can Cause Brain Damage, Scans Suggest." CBC. November 28, 2006. Retrieved August 2007 (http://www. cbc.ca/health/story/2006/11/28/ecstasy-brain.html).

Spicuzza, Mary. "Nightly Grind." Metroactive. March 23, 2000. Retrieved August 2007 (http://www.metroactive.com/papers/metro/ 03.23.00/ecstasy1-0012.html).

"Study Finds Long-Term Ecstasy Use Leads to Memory Loss." Narconon of Southern California. Retrieved August 2007 (http://www.ecstasy. ws/user-news.htm?id=126).

"Survey: Teens See Little Risk in Ecstasy." CNN.com. March 2, 2004. Retrieved August 2007 (http://www.cnn.com/2003/HEALTH/ parenting/02/11/drug.survey/index.html).

"Warning Over 'Rogue' Ecstasy." BBC News. August 9, 2000. Retrieved August 2007 (http://news.bbc.co.uk/1/hi/scotland/872272.stm).

"What Is Ecstasy?" InTheKnowZone.com. 2001. Retrieved August 2007 (http://www.intheknowzone.com/ecstasy/chemistry.htm).

Index

About the Author

Tamra Orr is the author of almost 100 nonfiction books for people of all ages. She lives in the Pacific Northwest and is the mother of four children. Her oldest child works for social services and shares with Orr sad and agonizing stories about the drug-addicted clients she deals with on a daily basis. With this insight into the lives of drug addicts and her in-depth research on related topics like ecstasy, Orr has become a strong advocate for understanding the power of drugs in today's culture and finding ways to keep the world's children safe from becoming statistics on the nightly news.

Photo Credits

Cover, p. 1 © www.istockphoto.com/Roberta Osborne; pp. 3, 9, 10, 26, 39, 41, 43, 44, 47 Courtesy of the U.S. Drug Enforcement Administration; p. 6 © Time & Life Pictures/Getty Images; p. 11 © Paolo Siccardi/age fotostock; pp. 12, 18, 33 © AP Images; p. 15 © Thomas Boyd/Zuma Press; p. 16 © Alfred Pasieka/Photo Researchers, Inc.; pp. 19, 22 © Getty Images; p. 24 © Scott Houston/Sygma/Corbis; p. 27 © www.istockphoto.com/stockphoto4u; p. 29 © John Bavosi/Photo Researchers, Inc.; p. 37 © Leilani Hu/Zuma Press; p. 38 © AFP/Getty Images.

Designer: Les Kanturek; **Photo Researcher:** Cindy Reiman